Sharks

Diane Swanson

Gareth Stevens Publishing
A WORLD ALMANAC EDUCATION GROUP COMPANY

Please visit our web site at: www.garethstevens.com
For a free color catalog describing Gareth Stevens Publishing's list of high-quality books
and multimedia programs, call 1-800-542-2595 (USA) or 1-800-387-3178 (Canada).
Gareth Stevens Publishing's fax: (414) 332-3567.

The publishers acknowledge the support of the Canada Council for the Arts and the Cultural Services
Branch of the Government of British Columbia in making this publication possible.

Library of Congress Cataloging-in-Publication Data

Swanson, Diane, 1944-
    [Welcome to the world of sharks]
    Sharks / by Diane Swanson. — North American ed.
      p. cm. — (Welcome to the world of animals)
    Includes index.
    Summary: An introduction to the physical characteristics, behavior, habitat, and life cycle
of sharks.
    ISBN 0-8368-3563-8 (lib. bdg.)
    1. Sharks—Juvenile literature. [1. Sharks.] I. Title.
QL638.9.S924   2003
597.3—dc21   2002030285

This edition first published in 2003 by
Gareth Stevens Publishing
A World Almanac Education Group Company
330 West Olive Street, Suite 100
Milwaukee, WI 53212 USA

This U.S. edition © 2003 by Gareth Stevens, Inc. Original edition © 2001 by Diane Swanson.
First published in 2001 by Whitecap Books, Vancouver. Additional end matter © 2003
by Gareth Stevens, Inc.

Series editors: Lauren Fox, Betsy Rasmussen
Design: Katherine A. Goedheer
Cover design: Renee M. Bach

Cover photograph: Kelvin Aitken/First Light
Photo credits: Neil G. McDaniel Photography 4, 8, 10, 20, 26, 28; David Doubilet/First Light 6; Nick
Caloyianis 12, 14, 18, 30; David Fleetham/First Light 16; K. Aitken/First Light 22; Graeme Eisenhofer 24

Printed in the United States of America

1 2 3 4 5 6 7 8 9 07 06 05 04 03

 # Contents

World of Difference

Sharks rule the sea. They are top-notch hunters with few enemies — but it's no wonder. Most sharks are master swimmers, able to charge powerfully through the water. And they possess a set of super senses for finding food and dodging danger.

Worldwide, there are 350 to 400 different kinds of sharks, and more than 100 kinds spend time off the coasts of Canada, the United States, and Mexico. Biggest of all are the whale sharks. They can be as long as two or three cars placed end to end! One of the smallest sharks is the cigar shark, a deepwater fish that is only about

A large school of scalloped hammer- heads gathers in warm waters.

A diver approaches a slow-swimming whale shark. As big as it is, it doesn't eat people.

the length of a cigar. In most shark families, females are larger than males.

Sharks usually come in dull colors, such as gray-blue and gray-green. That makes them hard to spot from above or below, which helps them hunt and stay clear of enemies.

Many sharks are shaped like rockets. Angel sharks, however, have flat bodies like skates and rays, the shark's close relatives. Sawsharks have long, sawlike snouts with sharp teeth along the edges. And hammerhead sharks have heads shaped like hammers, with eyes and nostrils at both ends of the "hammers."

You can usually find a shark's wide, curved mouth beneath its head — but not always. The strange frill shark, for example, has a mouth that's more like a snake's — right out in front.

SHARK SMARTS

Sharks are smart and can learn as fast as rats can. Some have mastered tricks, such as slipping hoops over their heads to get treats from their trainers. Others have figured out how to find their way through mazes.

Lemon sharks have even learned how to hit targets with their noses, making bells go off, then swimming to another spot to be fed. Over time, these sharks linked eating to the sound of the bells and swam directly to their feeding spot when they heard ringing.

Where in the World

Oceans everywhere are home to sharks. Different kinds of sharks live in different parts of the world, but more kinds live in warm water than cold. Some prefer shallow water, while others prefer the deep sea. Some stay close to coasts, and others swim in the open ocean. And bull sharks can live part of their lives in freshwater, such as the Mississippi River.

Angel sharks spend a lot of their time flat on the seafloor. They hide in sand that is the color of their skin. Divers who spot them rarely see more than the sharks' eyes, which sit on the top of their heads.

A nurse shark can breathe without swimming. On the seafloor, it just opens and closes its mouth.

Traveling from deep, dark waters, a sixgill shark can rise swiftly toward the surface.

During the day, swell sharks rest in underwater caves or narrow openings between rocks. They wedge themselves in place by swallowing a lot of water, making their bodies swell.

Occasionally, several swell sharks pile on top of one another. Being wedged into a hiding place probably helps protect them from enemies, such as larger sharks.

Many sharks spend time traveling every day or every season. They are constantly on the move to find more food or water temperatures that suit them. Female sharks often search for good nurseries — protected places for their young.

Some sharks move up and down between the deep and shallow waters of the sea. Others swim from one coast to another.

COMING UP IN THE WORLD

In most parts of the world, scientists have to board submersibles to study sixgill sharks. These ancient fish normally live 5,000 to 8,000 feet (1,500 to 2,500 meters) down.

But each year, some sixgill sharks visit a few spots along North America's west coast, often coming within 33 feet (10 meters) of the surface! Then scuba divers can swim with the sharks. Why these sixgills leave their deep-sea homes is a mystery no one has solved.

World in Motion

Swimming is what sharks do best. Streamlined bodies and coverings of special scales let them slip easily through the water. And unlike most other fish, sharks have skeletons made of cartilage, not bone. Cartilage is the material that shapes your ears and the tip of your nose. A cartilage skeleton bends easily and floats well, so sharks can move through the water with little effort.

Swimming power comes mostly from a shark's long tail and tail fins, which also help it make sudden turns. A thresher shark can use its tail — which is as long as its

Besides being able to swim across oceans, the blue shark can dive deep.

13

A basking shark moves slowly, straining the water for food.

body — to herd and stun fish for food. The one or two fins on a shark's back, plus a pair near its back end, help keep it upright in water. It uses its winglike side fins for steering.

Not all sharks swim fast. Big basking sharks and whale sharks just poke along as they feed near the ocean's surface. But the shortfin mako, one of the fastest sharks, can travel 22 miles (35 kilometers) per hour. The great white shark normally cruises slowly, saving its energy for short, high-speed attacks. When racing, a great white shark can leap right out of the water.

Some sharks are known for their long-distance swimming, not their speed. Blue sharks, for example, often make long trips. One swam all the way from New York to Brazil — a journey of about 3,725 miles (6,000 kilometers)!

MONSTER EXPOSED!

Some monsters in sea tales may really be basking sharks. Imagine as many as fifty of these giants — almost as long as whale sharks — sailing nose to tail. With only their top fins and a bit of their backs showing above water, they can appear to be one HUGE beast!

People also tell tales about dead basking sharks washing up on shore. Because their heads are small for their bodies, the sharks are often thought to be sea monsters.

World of Senses

Not much gets past a shark. Its senses are among the keenest of any animal. Although it has no outer ears, a shark hears well with its inner ears. Sound travels faster and farther through water than through air, so a shark can hear an injured seal or fish thrashing in the ocean more than a mile (1.5 kilometers) away.

Because shark nostrils aren't used for breathing, they work full-time at sniffing. They can smell food that is as far away as a few city blocks. Just a faint whiff of blood can attract a hungry shark's attention.

Like other fish, a shark has a narrow canal on each side of its head and body.

Sniff, sniff. The large nostrils of a sandbar shark draw smells from the water.

With clawlike parts, a copepod hooks onto the eye of a Greenland shark and feeds.

Tiny hairs in these canals sense small movements and changes in pressure. They help the shark keep its balance and tell direction. They also work with its other senses, especially hearing, to find food.

No one is sure how far sharks can see, but they are able to use their eyes when it's light and dark. In dim light, their sight probably works better than a cat's.

Sensors in hundreds of pores on the front of a shark's head detect electricity, which all animals produce. As the shark closes in on prey, it puts these sensors to work, even finding fish hidden in sand.

Some sharks also have feelers on their snouts for locating and tasting food. Taste buds in their mouths and throats help sharks decide whether to swallow or spit out the food they catch.

DEEP-SEA HITCHHIKERS

Tiny animals called copepods sometimes attach themselves to the eyes of Greenland sharks. As a copepod nibbles and scrapes an eye, it damages the sight of the shark.

The news isn't all bad for the shark, however. Because it lives mostly in the deep, dark waters of the Arctic and northern Atlantic Oceans, it doesn't depend much on its sight. The copepod might even attract fish that try to eat it. Then the Greenland shark can nab the fish.

Toothy World

Sharks have teeth outside as well as inside. Their skin is covered with tiny scales, called denticles, that are built like teeth. These denticles are so sharp that they can scrape patches of skin off of animals that rub against them. Throughout the shark's life, when the denticles break or fall out, they are quickly replaced.

Besides denticles, a shark grows a mouthful of teeth that vary according to the kind of shark it is. The teeth can be large or small, pointed or flat, smooth or rough, sharp or dull. Whale sharks have thousands of little, back-curving teeth set

This mouth was made for chomping! The great white shark has strong jaws and sharp teeth.

21

New, curved teeth form in the jaw of a tiger shark. The teeth can bite through turtle shells.

in more than three hundred rows. Great whites have long, pointed teeth with edges like bread knives. And cookie-cutter sharks — just the length of your arm — have teeth so sharp they have left marks on submarines!

Some sharks have combinations of different types of teeth. Bullhead sharks, for example, have small, sharp front teeth for grabbing fish and big, dull back teeth for crushing the shells of animals such as sea urchins.

Heavy-duty chomping can damage teeth, but that's no problem for a shark. Missing or broken teeth are replaced with spare ones that are always ready to move into place. During its lifetime, a shark might lose and replace as many as thirty thousand teeth! Like denticles, these teeth do not grow larger, but each time they are replaced, the new ones are a size bigger.

SCALES TELL TALES

Teeth and denticles are often all that are left of sharks that lived a long time ago. During the 1990s, some of the oldest denticles ever found were discovered in sandstone in Colorado. Each was less than one-twenty-fifth of an inch (one millimeter) long.

Scientists who examined the tiny denticles think they are probably about 450 million years old. They might have belonged to ancient sharks that had sucker-like mouths — instead of jaws — equipped with little teeth.

World Full of Food

Opening w-i-d-e is no trouble for a shark. Its jaws are loosely attached, making it easy for them to seize chunks of food. But the jaws don't move from side to side, so a shark cannot chew its dinner. Instead, many sharks swallow food, such as fish, whole, and they bite pieces off bigger animals.

What a shark eats depends a lot on its teeth. The tiny teeth of whale sharks cannot pierce food, so these fish feed on small plants and animals floating in the water. The sharp teeth and strong jaws of cookie-cutter sharks can clamp onto the sides of animals as large as whales. These

Whitetip reef sharks near Mexico gobble up fish and pull octopuses from their dens.

This spiny dogfish shark might eat a dinner of fish, squid, and worms — or become a dinner for seals or people.

sharks earn their name by twisting and turning to remove circles of flesh.

Most sharks feed on several kinds of animals, such as fish and octopuses. Some sharks nab whatever they can — even turtles and birds. Sharks can push their stomachs out through their mouths to throw up what they cannot digest, such as turtle shells or quickly swallowed cans!

When they can, sharks may choose one food over another. Hammerheads prefer stingrays, and basking sharks like plankton — tiny plants and animals floating in the water. Despite tales of great white sharks hunting people, humans aren't their usual or favorite food.

Many sharks feed alone, but some sharks hunt for food in packs. Thousands of spiny dogfish sharks, for example, may attack a school of cod.

FILTERING FOOD

The sharks with the biggest mouths eat the smallest food. Whale, basking, and mega-mouth sharks strain floating plants and animals — such as shrimp and copepods — from the sea. The sharks open their mouths and let the water flow in. The water passes back out through "sieves" in the sharks' gills, where the food sticks until it is swallowed.

In only an hour, a basking shark can strain the plants and animals from 2,000 tons (1,800 tonnes) of water!

New World

Shallow water can make good nurseries — warm places rich with food for young sharks, called pups. When it's time to lay egg cases or give birth, many female sharks head for these nurseries.

Only a few sharks lay egg cases. Horn sharks anchor tough, screw-shaped cases in cracks between rocks. Swell sharks deposit purselike cases among seaweed. When swell shark pups are ready to hatch, they use special denticles to free themselves.

Many shark pups hatch from eggs that are kept inside their mothers. The little sharks feed on their own egg yolks until

This brown cat shark — as long as a human arm — once hatched from an egg case the length of a human nose.

29

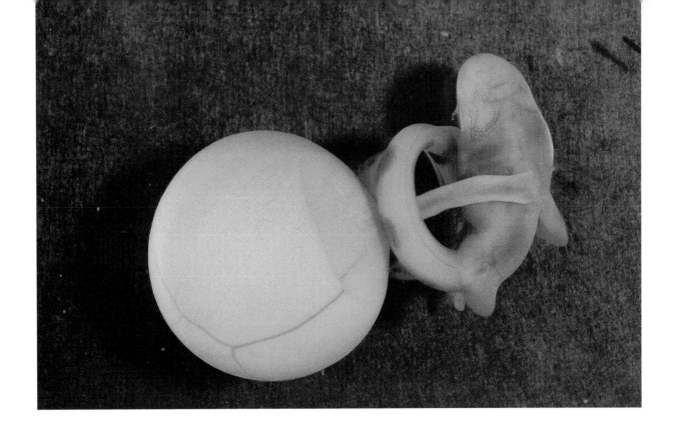

Using nutrients from an attached yolk sac, a shark pup develops inside its egg case.

they are ready to be born. Some kinds, such as sand tiger sharks, also feed on their brothers and sisters before birth!

Hammerhead, blue, and bull sharks carry their pups inside them — like mammals do. Until they are born, these pups are attached to their mother, getting all the nutrients they need from her.

Some sharks produce only one pup at a time. Others have many more. In 1995, scientists were shocked to find three hundred pups growing inside a captured whale shark.

As soon as they are born, shark pups care for themselves. They're quite large and well developed. They can swim strongly enough to find food and escape danger. The pups grow up slowly, and it is usually years before they are old enough to produce pups of their own.

SUPER SHARKS

Sharks are amazing! Here are just some of the reasons why:

- **Shortfin mako sharks can leap about 20 feet (6 meters) out of the water.**

- **Shark skin is rough enough to be used as sandpaper and tough enough to be made into leather boots.**

- **Most sharks live fewer than twenty-five years, but some spiny dogfish sharks might survive for one hundred years.**

Glossary

cartilage — the tough, rubbery white material that forms part of the skeleton of animals with backbones.

denticles — the pointed scales that cover a shark's body.

fins — thin, flat parts that project from a fish's body and are used for movement and balance.

gills — the body parts of a fish used to take oxygen from the water.

nurseries — places where eggs or young animals are cared for.

nutrients — parts of food needed for energy or growth and development.

pups — the babies or young of sharks and some other animals.

sensors — parts of the body that respond to taste, smell, sound, light, or other stimulation.

streamlined — shaped or built in a smooth, curved way that makes moving through water or air easier.

submersibles — submarines or other underwater vehicles, often used for deep-sea research.

Index